j551.447 Gallant, Roy A.
GAL
            Limestone caves.

$22.00

Limestone CAVES

by Roy A. Gallant

A First Book
Franklin Watts
A Division of Grolier Publishing
New York London Hong Kong Sydney
Danbury, Connecticut

Photographs ©: Animals Animals: 35 (Bertram G. Murray, Jr.), 37 (Klaus Uhlenhut); Earth Scenes: 11 top (Zig Leszcczynski), 25 bottom (T. Middleton), 27 (Alastair Shay); Gamma-Liaison: 45, 53 (Jerome Chatin); K.R Downey Photography: cover, 1, 4, 8, 14, 21, 29, 50; National Geographic: 47 (Sisse Brimberg), 28, 30 top, 52 (Michael K. Nichols); Peter Arnold Inc.: 32 (S. J. Krasemann); Norbert Wu: 17 (Peter Parks); Photo Researchers: 6, 20, 40 (Brian Blake), 39 (Suzanne L. Collins), 48 (De Sazo); 30 bottom (Jeff Lepore), 38 (Tom McHugh), 12 (Bruce Roberts); Tony Stone Images: 7 (Robert Frerck); UPI/Corbis-Bettmann: 42; Visuals Unlimited: 26, 22, 25 top (A. J. Copley), 11 bottom (John Gerlach), 31, 55 (William Palmer).

Library of Congress Cataloging-in-Publication Data

Gallant, Roy A.
    Limestone caves / by Roy A. Gallant.
       p. cm. — (A First book)
    Includes bibliographical references and index.
    Summary: Describes types of caves, particularly the formation and physical features of limestone caves, and provides information about the animal and plant life found in caves, as well as about human cave dwellers and their paintings.
    ISBN 0–531–20293–3 (lib. bdg.)   0-531-15910-8 (pbk.)
    1. Caves—Juvenile literature. 2. Limestone—Juvenile literature. [1. Caves.] I. Title. II. Series.
    GB601.2.G34 1998
    551.41'7—dc21   97–3467
                                                      CIP
                                                       AC

Content

Caves come in all sizes
from narrow tunnels to
huge caverns.

Introduction

Caves are natural openings in the ground. While some are as small as a telephone booth, others are enormous caverns the size of a house or a hotel. Still others are a maze of passageways many miles long. The corridors and tunnels of Kentucky's Mammoth Cave wind and loop like a giant pretzel for more than 300 miles (483 kilometers).

There are caves in just about every part of the world. Jean Bernard Cave in France is currently thought to be the deepest cave on Earth. From its highest opening, this cave tunnels 5,256 feet (1,602 meters) underground. The deepest cave in the continental United States is Lechuguilla Cave in New Mexico. It is 1,565 feet (477 m) deep. The United States has approximately 17,000 caves. Most are "wild" caves, meaning they do not offer guided tours for tourists. But more than 200 are "show caves," complete with colored lights and guided tours along walkways or by boat on underground streams.

Most caves have been around for a very long time. When you step into a cave you may be entering an ancient world a few million years old. The cave may even have been a home for people living more than 30,000 years ago. Evidence of ancient cave dwellers has been found in many parts of the world—including Asia, Africa, South America, France, Spain, and Israel. In some caves, we find the bones of animals that ended up in one of their cooking pots. Other caves were used as burial places, storehouses, and places of worship. On the walls and ceiling of some caves, we see figures of

Show caves, such as Luray Caverns in Virginia, feature lights, walkways, and guided tours.

In 1879, a Spanish nobleman discovered the first known prehistoric paintings on the ceiling of Altamira cave in northeast Spain. These paintings, including the bison pictured here, are about 14,000 years old

animals and humans painted long ago by prehistoric artists.

Although few people live in caves today, many animals do. Biologists have found thousands of kinds of animals that spend their entire lives in the total darkness of caves. Many such animals are blind because countless generations of their ancestors have known only darkness. Some do not have eyes at all. Bats and a number of larger animals live in caves only part of the time, or they may use a cave as an emergency shelter. For many scientists, caves are natural laboratories where they can study the formation of caves, observe many fascinating rock and mineral formations, examine the life histories of rare animals, and learn more about the lives of ancient people.

A lava tube in Bend, Oregon

Chapter 1

Kinds of Caves

There are four major types of caves: *lava tubes, sea caves, sandstone caves,* and *solution caves.*

Lava tubes are shaped like subway tunnels. They form from a river of molten lava that flows out of a volcano. In the open air, the exposed surface of the lava flow cools and gradually solidifies. Meanwhile, the hot lava inside keeps flowing, like water through a pipe. When the volcano stops erupting, the hot lava eventually drains out of the hardened exterior, leaving a long cave. The entrance to a lava tube is not at the end of the tube. Instead, it is a hole in the tube's ceiling where a weak section of tube has collapsed. Lava caves may be several miles long and more than 30 feet (9 m) across. Sometimes, other tubes branch off the main tube. There are many lava tubes in the western United States and Hawaii.

Sea caves are found along the shores of oceans and large lakes. They are formed by hundreds or thousands of years of wave action. Over time, as powerful waves batter a rock cliff, the pounding water breaks away weak and loose pieces of rock. Sand and gravel carried by the water help chip away at the rock, like millions of tiny hammers. Eventually a cave forms, and it keeps getting larger until it is beyond the reach of the waves. The Pacific coast of the United States features many sea caves. The world's largest sea cave, Sea Lion Caves in Oregon, is as high as a twelve-story building and as long as a football field. It is home to about 200 sea lions.

Sandstone caves are shallow, hollowed-out cavities in the base of cliffs made of a soft rock called sandstone. As rainwater or water from a stream flows down the face of a sandstone cliff, it *dissolves* some of the cementing chemical that holds together the sand grains that make up the rock. The water then washes away some of the sand and gradually carves out a cave. Ancient people who lived in caves preferred sandstone caves to all other types. Colorado's Mesa Verde National Park features many excellent examples of sandstone shelter caves.

The fourth major cave type, and the one of most interest to us in this book, is called a solution cave. Solution caves outnumber all other cave types, and many people think they are the most interesting and spectacular. They are found only in certain kinds of

Sea Lion Caves

Cliff Palace, in Mesa Verde National Park, was built in the shelter of a huge sandstone cave. An American Indian people known as the Anasazi (a Navajo word meaning "ancient ones") constructed Cliff Palace around 1200 and lived there for 75 to 100 years.

rock. These rocks include limestone, dolomite, marble, and gypsum.

Over hundreds of thousands of years, water in the ground trickles down through cracks in the underlying rock. Ever so slowly, the rock is weakened and dissolved away by the water. Eventually, small tunnels form in the rock. The tunnels then enlarge and become irregular passages. As more rock dissolves, some of the passages become large caverns with truly beautiful and spectacular rock and crystal formations. Not only do solution caves outnumber all other cave types, they are the world's largest caves. Let's find out how one particular kind of solution cave—called a limestone cave—is formed.

The park ranger seems very small in this huge cavern, aptly named the Big Room (Carlsbad Caverns, New Mexico).

Spectacular limestone formations in
Lechuguilla Cave, New Mexico

Chapter 2

How Limestone Caves Form

Man-made "caves" such as subway tunnels, or tunnels under a river or through a mountain, are marvels of modern-day technology. The engineers who build them work as fast as they can. Using clattering jackhammers, giant boring machines, powerful explosives, and bulldozers, workers can tunnel through more than 7,000 feet (2,134 m) of solid rock in a little more than two months.

Nature, however, hollows out a limestone tunnel silently, and ever so slowly. Its only tool is water, and the job may take millions of years. But unlike tunnel engineers, nature has all the time in the world. Most large limestone caves are at least a million years old. Such a cave may last for a few million more years, but eventually it will be destroyed when its roof collapses.

Limestone comes in many forms. One type of limestone you've seen is blackboard chalk, but limestone caves form only in harder types of limestone. Limestone usually forms at the bottom of a shallow sea. It is made of the mineral *calcite.*

Countless tiny ocean organisms have skeletons made of calcite. Most of these organisms are so small that you need a microscope to see them. Over millions of years, these organisms are born and die. As they die, a gentle rain of their skeletons drifts to the seafloor and forms a carpet of calcite. The carpet thickens as more and more skeletons pile up. Eventually, after millions of years, the calcite carpet may become hundreds of feet thick and hundreds of miles wide.

Layers of sand and mud may build up on top of the calcite carpet. Meanwhile, the weight of the ocean water, as well as overlying layers of sand and mud, compresses the calcite. At the same time, minerals seep into the tiny spaces between the microscopic calcite particles and cement them together. Eventually, the calcite hardens into limestone.

And there the limestone may remain for millions of years. There are a few ways for the limestone to emerge from the sea. The sea level may drop and expose the limestone to light and air, though it may still be covered by other layers of rock that have built up on top of it. Alternatively, powerful forces deep within the earth may thrust up the limestone seabed and raise it above the surface of the sea. In either case, the limestone is now ready for the long process of cave formation to begin.

These microscopic shells, greatly magnified here, form
a carpet of calcite as they collect on the seafloor.

The age of the limestone and the age of the cave
carved out of the limestone are not the same. Caves are
always much younger than the limestone they are
carved in. Most are probably not older than about 10
million years. The process of carving a limestone cave
begins with rain. As raindrops fall through the air, they
capture *carbon dioxide* gas. Carbon dioxide is the waste

gas we breathe out. It is also given off by the remains of dead plants. When the rain soaks into the soil, it picks up still more carbon dioxide. As rain picks up carbon dioxide, the water turns into a weak acid called *carbonic acid*. This acid can actually dissolve, or eat its way through, limestone.

The acid water soaks through the soil, and in areas where limestone lies beneath the surface, the water then seeps down through cracks in the rock. Eventually it reaches a layer of limestone where the cracks and pores are already filled with water. The upper limit of this vast underground water source is called the *water table*. The water beneath the water table is called *groundwater*.

Not too long ago, geologists (scientists who study the earth) supposed that solution caves were scoured out by the action of fast underground streams, in much the way valleys are carved by the flow of rivers. But their thinking has changed in recent years.

Geologists now think that cave formation takes place just below the water table. All the limestone below the water table is soaked with the acid water. As the water slowly moves through this soaked zone of rock, it gradually eats away at the limestone and forms water-filled cavities and passageways. But why does it carve out only cavities and passageways instead of dissolving all of the rock?

One reason is that the limestone is often mixed

with other rock types, and the acid groundwater can dissolve only the limestone. So a zigzagging passageway represents the space once filled mostly with limestone and not the other, more resistant rock types. Another reason is that the water may tend to flow through fractures in the rock, dissolving only the limestone near the fractures. The fractures then widen into cave passageways.

Eventually, the land surface dips down to where it meets the water table, and the slow-moving groundwater reaches the surface as a spring. Or it may drain into a stream or river. The flow of groundwater is very slow, usually less than 33 feet (10 m) a year.

The next stage in limestone cave formation seems to be a lowering of the water table. This can be caused by climate change such as a lack of rain. Alternatively, this drop in the water table can occur over centuries as a nearby river cuts deeper into its bed and so deepens the valley around it. The deepening of the river valley then drains away more of the surrounding groundwater and so lowers the water table.

As the water table drops, groundwater drains out of the cavities and passageways it had formed over many centuries. Eventually, air breaks into the passageways. A cave has been formed. For centuries to come, a cave may have a slow-moving river flowing through it until the water table lowers enough to drain out the last of the groundwater.

As a river cuts deeper into a valley, the water table may lower, draining groundwater out of caves.

In any case, once air breaks into the cavity, the cave stops growing larger. This happens even though water may still be flowing through part of it. As soon as air enters the cave, much of the carbon dioxide in the remaining water escapes into the air, just as carbon dioxide gas escapes from a soda bottle when it is opened. The water loses so much carbon dioxide that it is no longer acidic enough to dissolve the limestone. But

This cave, like all solution caves, was once entirely filled with water. Air has broken into this cave, but only some of the water has drained out.

something else happens as well.

As the groundwater becomes less acidic, it can no longer hold the calcite that was dissolved in the water. The calcite in the water then begins to *precipitate*—it becomes solid and separates from the water. This marks the most interesting stage in the formation of a limestone cave. The process that carved the cave out of limestone now goes into reverse—the water that had dissolved the calcite in the limestone now deposits solid calcite back into the cave. Splendid calcite formations begin to take shape. The ceiling and floor of the cave become decorated with spectacular structures that include *stalagmites*, *stalactites*, *gypsum flowers*, *cave pearls*, and *cave cotton*.

Newly forming stalactites are sometimes called "soda straws."

Chapter 3

Features of Limestone Caves

When limestone cave formation ceases, the creative chemical processes that decorate the cave begin. The resulting features include forests of stalactites, stalagmites, gypsum flowers, columns, flowstone, rimstone dams, hanging curtains of stone, and other colorful features of cave architecture.

Stalactites usually are the first to form. They begin when calcite-rich water drips out of cracks in the cave ceiling. The calcite in the dripwater precipitates from the water, leaving a trace of hardened calcite on the ceiling. Each drop of water adds a little more calcite to the growing stalactite, forming a tiny, delicate tube. It looks a bit like a hanging soda straw.

This tube stage is a critical time in the formation of a stalactite because the tubes are extremely delicate. Sometimes they break away from the cave ceiling under their own weight. In Soldiers Cave, California, a patch of soft soil has a group of fallen tube stalactites sticking out of it like arrows. At some point in the past, they broke away from the ceiling.

Over time, a young stalactite's hollow tube fills in. Calcite-rich water from the ceiling then creeps down the outside of the stalactite, broadening it at its base where it joins the ceiling and lengthening it. It starts to look like an icicle of stone. Stalactites grow very slowly, usually only a small fraction of an inch (2 millimeters or so) a year.

As water drips off a growing stalactite, it splashes on the cave floor. Here again, the water drops leave behind a very small amount of calcite. This gradually forms a mound of rock on the cave floor. Drip by drip, the mound slowly grows into an upside-down icicle of stone pointing upward exactly beneath the downward-pointing stalactite. These formations are called stalagmites. They are usually thicker than the stalactites above them because the splash from the falling drops of calcite-rich water forms a wider base platform for the growing stalagmite.

Stalagmites often grow to be more than 50 feet (15 m) high and 33 feet (10 m) across at their base. They usually have rounded tips. When dripwater falls onto a growing stalagmite from a great height, however, the splash may cause the top of the stalagmite to be flat or even bowl-shaped. Stalagmites grow at about the same speed as stalactites. Geologists who measured the

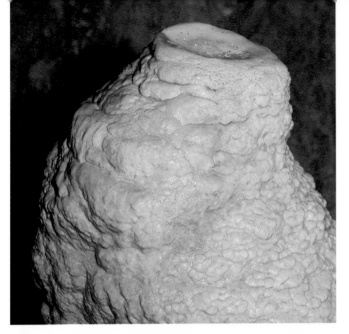

Water splashing on top of this stalagmite has formed a bowl-shaped tip, called a splash cup.

Stalagmites build up as water drips off the stalactites above them. Eventually the stalagmite may join the stalactite directly above, forming a column.

A giant stalactite and stalagmite have joined to form this huge column in the King's Palace room of Carlsbad Caverns.

growth rate of stalagmites in Moaning Cave, California, found one that took 1,400 years to grow 3.5 inches (8.8 cm).

Century after century, the downward-pointing tip of a driping stalactite closes the gap between itself and the upward-pointing tip of the stalagmite beneath. Eventually, the two tips may join. When they do, the calcite-rich water creeping down the stalactite thickens the two joined structures into a *column*. Columns can grow to be more than 60 feet (18 m) high and 30 feet (9 m) wide.

Stalactites, stalagmites, and columns are all known as *speleothems*. A speleothem is any structure, usually made of calcite, that forms from water dripping through a solution cave. There are many other kinds of speleothems. One type of speleothem, called a *drapery*, is very delicate. Draperies are thin sheets of calcite that hang from a cave ceiling. They may grow to be more than 10 feet (3 m) long, and some draperies are so thin you can see right through them. They look a little like window draperies.

A drapery begins to form when a drop of calcite-rich water flows down along a slightly sloping ceiling. As it does, it leaves behind a tiny trail of calcite. One drop follows another, and another, and another until the thin calcite trail builds downward from the ceiling, one layer on another for thousands of years. A newly-forming drapery is no thicker than the drops of water forming it.

As the water soaks through the soil above the limestone cave, it picks up various minerals. These minerals may color the water orange, yellow, or brown. As the water soaks down through the ground and drips into the cave, the colored water may form colored draperies.

Over the long period of time it takes for a drapery to form, the kinds of minerals in the soil above the limestone cave can change. As a result, some draperies are streaked with many different colors, like a piece of ribbon candy.

Dripwater in a limestone cave sometimes flows down a section of a cave's walls or floor. As it does, it forms thin sheets of calcite

Minerals in the water that formed this drapery have given it colored stripes.

The huge flowstone deposit on the floor of this cave looks like a river of rock. The cave explorer has removed his boots to avoid soiling the flowstone.

called *flowstone*. The ripples in some flowstone formations give the impression that the rock is flowing through the cave.

Pools of water and slowly flowing streams often cover the floors of limestone caves. Some of the pools are bordered by fencelike deposits of calcite. Called *rimstone dams*, these speleothems often form in steplike fashion along a sloping cave floor, each dam holding a pool of water. The water flows and tumbles from one pool to the next lower one. Some rimstone dams are only a fraction of an inch, or a few millimeters, high. Others may build to heights of 3 feet (90 centimeters) or more.

Not everyone agrees on how rimstone dams form, but some scientists offer this explanation. The water flowing along a cave floor is shaken up whenever it jumps along a small rapids. As the water is shaken, it loses some dissolved calcite, which is deposited on the floor as a small ridge. This ridge accumulates more and more calcite, and the dam grows higher.

A cave explorer studies a series of rimstone dams.

Perhaps the rarest cave features of all are cave pearls, such as those found in Carlsbad Caverns and Lechuguilla Cave, New Mexico. Cave pearls are round speleothems that lie freely on the cave floor. They range in size from a fraction of an inch to several inches across. While the smaller cave pearls usually are ball shaped, larger ones are more often irregular lumps. But a nearly perfectly shaped cave pearl almost 3 inches (8 cm) across and weighing 2 pounds (0.9 kilograms) was found in Virginia's Carpenter Cave.

A cave pearl may start out as a grain of sand or a chip of rock resting on the ground beneath an area of dripwater. Sometimes the fragment rests in a pool of water fed by dripwater from above the pool. In either case, the fragment collects onionlike shells of calcite as water gently splashes against it. The larger well-

Cave pearls in
Lechuguilla Cave

rounded cave pearls seem to form in pools of water, where they are kept in motion and evenly build up shells of calcite.

Water that seeps slowly into a cave sometimes forms *helictites*, which are among the most beautiful and delicate cave features. These curled, twisted, or spiraling structures are usually a few inches long. They form on the walls, ceilings, and floors of caves. Although most helictites are made of calcite, some form from other minerals, such as aragonite. Virginia's Skyline Caverns have many aragonite helictites.

Almost every limestone cave in the world has *cave coral*, which also is formed by seeping water. The coral comes in small clusters of knobs. Some knobs are attached to the

These delicate helictites grow from the ceiling of Cave of the Winds in Colorado.

cave wall while others are attached to stems that stick out of the wall for 2 inches (5 cm) or more. Close relatives of cave coral are gypsum flowers. These are formed out of a mineral called gypsum. Gypsum flowers grow outward from their base, like toothpaste squeezed out of the tube. They grow into delicate forms shaped like flower petals and curling stems. Kentucky's Mammoth Cave contains rare gypsum flowers that grow more than 12 inches (30 cm) out from the cave wall.

Gypsum forms other speleothems as well. Geologist George Moore, of the U.S. Geological Survey, described another type of gypsum formation in these words: "Some caves contain filaments of gypsum so slender and threadlike that they wave like spider webs with each breath of air. Massive bunches of these filaments are called cave cotton."

There are still more limestone cave features, including cave blisters, cave rope, and cave bubbles. But descriptions of them could fill ten books this size. It's time now to find out about the strange living creatures that make caves their home.

A gypsum flower

31

At dusk, millions of free-tailed bats
emerge from Bracken Cave, Texas, in
search of food. During the night, the bats
will eat about 250 tons of insects. Bats
are very useful creatures to have around.

Chapter 4

Cave Life

Caves have been home to animals large and small for millions of years. Some biologists arrange cave creatures into three different groups: 1) ancient cave animals that have become extinct; 2) animals that spend only part of their lives in caves; and 3) animals that spend their entire lives in caves and never see the light of day. Let's look at each group.

Many ancient animals lived in caves. More than 35,000 years ago, there were cave lions, cave leopards, cave hyenas, and cave wolves. All were larger versions of their descendants living today. There were also many cave bears. Some were the size of today's grizzly bears, but other species were smaller than today's bears. We know about all these animals from their bones, which have been found on cave floors. These animals also appear in ancient paintings decorating cave walls in France, Spain, Brazil, and other parts of the world.

Today, many animals throughout the world spend part of their time in caves. Because deep caves usually stay about the same temperature summer and winter, they can provide animals with shelter from extreme weather. The temperature in most caves ranges from about 55°F to 65°F (13°C to 18°C). The general rule is that the temperature in a cave remains around the average yearly temperature of the region where the cave is located. So a deep cave offers a place to cool off on a hot summer day and a place to get warm on a cold winter day.

Bears often live in caves. Other animals that seek shelter near cave entrances are raccoons, snakes, rats, and a Central American animal called the spotted cavy. But the best-known cave dwellers are bats. Among them are the leaf-nose bat, the gray bat, the red bat, and the horseshoe bat, to name only four of about 1,000 different kinds of bats.

The world's largest bat colony lives in Bracken Cave near San Antonio, Texas. By day, about 20 million Mexican free-tailed bats cling to the ceiling of the cave. Most such cave bats are insect-eaters, hunting mosquitoes, centipedes, potato beetles, and other pests during the night. The floors of bat caves are covered with a slippery carpet of bat droppings, called *guano*. Guano is a rich natural fertilizer prized by farmers lucky enough to have a bat cave on their property.

At least two kinds of birds make their homes in

caves. One is the oilbird, or guacharo, of South America and Trinidad. It lives either in sea caves or caves in the mountains. Like a bat, it stays inside the cave during the day, flying outside only in the early evening in search of fruit.

Oilbirds in a cave in Trinidad,
an island off the coast of Venezuela

Another cave-dwelling bird is the swiftlet of Southeast Asia and Australia. It builds its nests in the deep interior of caves, often sharing them with bats. Both swiftlets and bats can fly in dark caves without flying into each other or the walls of the cave. The animals avoid mid-air collisions by uttering rapid and loud clicking signals. These sounds bounce off the surrounding objects and back to the bat or swiftlet, allowing the animal to sense obstructions in its path even in total darkness. This type of navigation is called *echolocation*. While bats leave the cave toward the end of day and stay away all night, the swiftlets use the cave overnight. In the morning the bats return, and the swiftlets leave for their daylight activity.

Another interesting thing about swiftlets is their unusual nest. It is made mostly or entirely of dried saliva from the bird's mouth. The Chinese regard the nests as a rare and expensive delicacy, and they use them to make a dish called bird's nest soup. Hong Kong is the world's headquarters for the collection and sale of swiftlet nests to restaurants and individuals. A Hong Kong restaurant may charge as much as $50 for one bowl of bird's nest soup. A bag of fifty or so nests sells for almost $1,000. Unfortunately, removing swiftlet nests disrupts the population of the birds. Some experts fear that this 1,500-year-old Chinese craving for bird's nest soup may soon wipe out the swiftlets as a species.

These swiftlets are nesting in a cave in eastern Australia. The nests are made mostly or entirely of the birds' saliva.

So far we have mentioned animals that spend only part of their lives in caves. But there are many others that rarely, if ever, see the light of day. In fact, some species of animals have lived in total darkness, generation after generation, for many thousands of years. Such animals include certain types of crickets, beetles, spiders, crayfish, centipedes, salamanders, and fish. And there is not a single vegetarian among them. Many cave creatures have eyes that do not see; some lack eyes altogether. The rule in nature is that if body organs, such as eyes, are not used, they may gradually disappear over many generations. Kentucky's Mammoth Cave has about 75 species of such blind creatures. Several hundred more such species have been found in European caves.

One of the more interesting blind cave dwellers is the 4-inch-long (10-cm-long) blindfish. It is colorless and has only traces of what were once eyes thousands of generations ago. Although it can't see, it is somehow sensitive to light, for it shuns even the dim light of a match. The animal's sense of touch is keen, as it is in most blind creatures. On the front and sides of its head, the blindfish has ridges of small projections that are sensitive to touch.

In the dark, underground world where this blindfish lives, eyes are of little use.

Certain types of salamanders also have adjusted to life in the dark and have come to lack working eyes. Some caves in southwestern Missouri contain blind salamanders that have never been found outside of caves. Blind crayfish also are common in the dark interior of some caves. One species is not only blind but is deaf as well.

Some creatures have extremely long legs and sensitive body hairs that enable them to sense their surroundings and swiftly detect predators. Blind beetles use very long antennae to grope their way through the

These blind salamanders
live in a cave in Texas.

darkness. Added to this zoo of blind and colorless animals are mites, primitive wingless insects, flies, and worms.

How did the blind cave creatures lose their sight? Scientists believe that the ancestors of today's blind animals lived outside of caves and had normal sight. These animals were somehow carried into caves, where they remained and reproduced. Since their eyes were of no use in the dark, they withered away over many generations.

Who eats what? Blindfish and crayfish eat mostly food brought into the cave by flowing water. Cave crickets eat mold that grows on bat guano and bird droppings. The crickets are food for cave beetles, centipedes, spiders, and insect-eating birds. Waitomo Cave in New Zealand is home to glowworms that light up the roof of the cave like a starry sky. Insects that float into the cave on a stream, or that drift into the cave on air currents, are attracted by the glow, captured, and eaten by the glowworms.

Earlier we said that caves long ago provided a home for people. Who were these people, and how do we know about them?

The glowworms on the ceiling of Waitomo Cave in New Zealand provide a spectacular sight for passengers on a guided boat tour.

Why would prehistoric artists decorate the walls of dark limestone caves?

Chapter 5

Limestone Cave Art

Some limestone caves feature ancient paintings made by prehistoric people. Who were the people who made these paintings? And why would people, some 30,000 years ago, have gone to the trouble to decorate the walls of dark caves with beautiful paintings of horses, bears, mammoths, panthers, and other animals?

We know the answer to the first question. But experts can't agree on an answer to the second one.

The people were cave dwellers who lived from about 35,000 to 10,000 years ago. Their remains have been found in many parts of the world. Many of them lived in sandstone caves carved out by water. These caves were not the deep, dark, and damp limestone caves where the paintings are found. The sandstone caves were just deep enough, and large enough, to provide shelter for a clan of people. These people used fire, gathered edible plants, and were expert hunters. They also made useful tools out of rock and bone. They lived in Europe, the Middle East, Africa, Australia, Siberia, Brazil, the American West and Southwest, and other parts of the world.

There are hundreds of known caves with paintings and engravings. More than 100 magnificently decorated caves have been discovered in Europe alone. Most of them are in France and Spain, and there probably are many more such caves waiting to be discovered. Most are limestone caves with large areas of smooth, white calcite walls. They probably were chosen by the cave artists because the walls provided an ideal surface for paintings.

The world's most famous art cave is Lascaux Cave in southwestern France. It was discovered accidentally by four boys in 1940. The boys found a small hole at the base of a tree. They were curious about the hole because they had heard that somewhere nearby a secret tunnel led to the basement of a famous old mansion. To find out how deep the hole was, they dropped in a few stones. They listened and heard the stones bounce and tumble down a long rock corridor.

Hoping to discover the secret tunnel, one of the boys had brought along an oil lamp. They decided to dig the hole wide enough to squeeze through. One by one they entered and climbed along the entrance passage to the cave's deep interior. Imagine their surprise when they entered a large cave room and the flickering light of their lamp revealed the most beautiful and colorful paintings of bulls and deer they had ever seen.

They reported their discovery, and almost overnight the Lascaux Cave became famous. Like a magnet, it attracted some of the world's leading archaeologists and art experts. As an adult, one of the cave's founders, Jacques Marsal, became the chief guide at the cave.

Two of Lascaux Cave's discoverers (center) pose at the cave's entrance with their schoolmaster (left) and an expert who has come to examine the paintings. The boy seated on the rock is Jacques Marsal, who later became the cave's chief guide.

The Lascaux paintings are about 17,000 years old. The cave consists of a large room called the Hall of the Bulls. It is 56 feet (17 m) long, 23 feet (7 m) wide, and the ceiling reaches a height of 20 feet (6 m). Two large passageways branch off from the main gallery.

More than fifty paintings of bulls—great beasts that weighed more than a ton—cover the ceilings and walls of the cave. Hundreds of horses and shaggy ponies with long winter coats appear on the bright calcite surfaces. Painted horses seem to walk along a path of dark limestone. Altogether, 600 paintings and 1,500 engravings of bulls, horses, ponies, cave lions, bison, cows, and great red deer decorate the ancient gallery. In addition, the prehistoric artists painted mysterious patterns of dots and rectangles among the animals.

The cave was not a living space but a place for painting and engraving, and a place where magic was performed. Tools and minerals that supplied the artists with the yellow, white, red, and black pigments have been found scattered throughout the cave. The style of the works suggests that all the paintings were done by just a few highly skilled artists, possibly by a master and his pupils. The people who did the paintings are known as *Magdalenians*, named after a region in France called La Madeleine. This group of people inhabited the region from about 18,000 to 11,000 years ago. Numerous other caves in France and Spain tell a similar story.

In December 1994, scientists discovered Cauvet

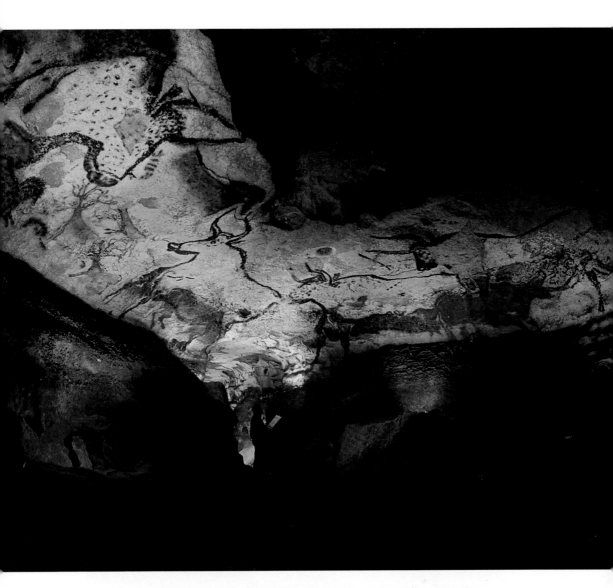

Large, stunning paintings of bulls, deer, and other animals
cover the ceiling and walls of the Hall of the Bulls.

Cave, the oldest known decorated cave. Also located in southwestern France, it has more than 300 beautiful paintings made by people living in the region about 33,000 years ago. The animals painted most often in this cave are woolly rhinoceroses, lions, and bears. In addition, there are mammoths, oxen, horses, and wild cats. There are also rare images of owls, a panther, and a hyena. And as at Lascaux, mysterious dots and rectangles are found. The painters of this cave left behind their footprints, bones of bears, charcoal from fires, and pieces of flint—a stone commonly used for making tools.

Deer heads in Lascaux Cave

Now we return to the second question at the beginning of this chapter: why did ancient people create these paintings?

Art experts and archaeologists can't agree on an answer, but they do have some ideas. It was once thought that the paintings were made to bring good luck to a tribe's hunters. Picturing a horse on the cave wall might aid the hunters in capturing a wild horse. Picturing a wounded deer with a spear sticking out of its side might help the hunters kill a deer. The paintings may have been done by a clan leader called a *shaman*.

Shamans were believed to be workers of magic and were much admired and feared by the people. Clan members believed that their tribal shaman had the power to communicate with the spirit world, to battle devils who would bring disease and other misfortunes to the clan.

Did ancient people believe that a shaman's power came from the cave paintings? Some historians think so. According to Jean Clottes, a French expert in art history and cave painting, "It looks to me like people produced many works of art in these caves as a means of traveling to a supernatural world."

Perhaps we will never know just why all those wondrous cave paintings were made or what purposes they served. Wherever the truth about their creation lies, they provide us with some of the most splendid examples of human creativity.

Many cave explorers find it difficult to adequately express the exhilaration of visiting the dreamlike world of a limestone cave.

Chapter 6

When You Visit a Cave

Fragile, exquisite, delicate, beautiful, wondrous. . . . There are not enough words to describe the breathtaking experience of visiting a limestone cave, whether it is decorated with the paintings of prehistoric people or with nature's own calcite speleothems. It is an experience that devoted cave explorers try to repeat as often as they can. So awesome is this underground dreamlike world, some people say they have become addicted to cave exploration.

There is a saying among dedicated cave explorers: "Take with you from a cave nothing but its photograph; leave nothing but your footprints." Some cavers even go to the trouble of wiping clean a stalactite that has been soiled by a muddy glove. Others will risk a dangerous fall by refusing to grab a stalactite for fear of breaking it. And some wear special nonmarking boots that leave hardly a trace of their footprints. And they

When visiting a cave, try to disturb the delicate cave environment as little as possible. This dedicated cave explorer in Lechuguilla Cave washes off a footprint left behind by an earlier expedition.

use tarps as a floor cloth to catch the crumbs of their lunch.

Compare that respectful and caring behavior with the behavior of some tourists who try to break off souvenir stalactites, delicate gypsum flowers, or other fragile cave decorations that have been forming for more than a million years.

However, no matter how well behaved and respectful of nature a visitor to a show cave may be, the visitor cannot help but change the cave in some small way. Pollen grains and dust may fall from clothing and so introduce substances from the outside into the cave. The light bulbs used to illuminate the colorful decorations of a show cave change the cave. The lighting enables green plants such as algae, mosses, and even ferns to grow in the cave. In some show caves, the growth of algae and moss on the cave walls has to be controlled.

Nowhere has the destructive intrusion of visitors to a cave been more obvious than in Lascaux Cave. Eight years after the cave's discovery, the French government opened the cave to visitors. Masons made a stairway into the cave and electricians arranged lights. Then the tourists came, at first about 600 a day. Before long, the tour guides began to complain of headache at the end of the day. So did some visitors. The reason was a buildup of carbon dioxide in the cave from the breathing of so many people. Carbon dioxide had built up to the point that it was hard to light a match.

Early visitors to Lascaux Cave upset the sensitive cave environment, jeopardizing the condition of the precious paintings. Today, conditions in the cave are monitored very carefully, and few visitors are allowed into the cave.

Body heat given off by the tourists caused a different problem. When body heat came in contact with the cool walls of the cave, it produced small droplets of water. As the water trickled down the cave walls, it washed away some of the paintings' color.

Expensive machinery was then set up in the cave to control the amount of moisture, the air temperature, and the amount of carbon dioxide. All was well, or so it seemed. Then, in the 1960s, even more tourists came to the cave—about 1,200 a day! Seeds, pollen, bacteria, and other germs flowed into the cave with the tourists. Soon, a guide noticed that tiny green spots had begun to appear on the cave walls. Algae, brought in by the tourists, had invaded the cave. The artificial lighting encouraged the algae growth.

Teams of experts examined the cave as if it were a dying patient. They ordered special disinfectant sprays to control the algae growth. They also ordered that the lighting be dimmed and that all visitors to the cave walk through a special shoe bath to help control the invasion of germs. Satisfied that the cave patient had been saved, the government decided to close the cave to tourists. The treasure of Lascaux was just too precious. Today the cave may be visited only by art historians, archaeologists, and other scholars who have been given special permission.

If you decide to visit one of the many show caves open to tourists, be respectful and you will not have a problem. But if you want to explore a privately owned cave, make certain to get permission and advice from the owner. And if you want to explore a wild cave, get in touch with the nearest cave "grotto." A "grotto" is a local chapter of the National Speleological Society. They will advise you about proper equipment and probably even supply you with a detailed map of the cave.

Exploring wild caves can be very dangerous. Never enter a wild cave without an experienced leader who is familiar with the cave. The rewards of safe cave exploration are tremendous. You may find fantastic speleothems and exotic animals. And perhaps you will help solve the mysteries about caves that still puzzle scientists around the world.

Many aspects of limestone caves are not yet understood by scientists. Perhaps you can help solve these mysteries.

Glossary

Algae—Green organisms as small as a single cell or larger.

Bacteria—Microscopic single-cell organisms.

Calcite—The chemical compound calcium carbonate ($CaCO_2$). It is composed of the skeletal remains of tiny sea organisms.

Carbon dioxide—A gas composed of carbon and oxygen (CO_2). It is the waste gas we exhale during breathing.

Carbonic acid—An acid (H_2CO_3) formed when rainwater picks up and dissolves carbon dioxide. It is the agent that dissolves limestone to form limestone caves.

Cave coral—Small clusters or knobs of calcite. Some are attached to a limestone cave's wall while others are attached to stems that stick out of the wall.

Cave cotton—Bunches of slender filaments of gypsum so fragile that they wave like spiderwebs with each breath of air.

Cave pearl—A pearl-like formation of calcite formed when calcite-rich dripwater gently splashes over a grain of rock and builds up layer after layer of the white mineral.

Column—The calcite formation formed wherever dripwater from a stalactite closes the gap between the stalactite tip and the stalagmite forming directly beneath. Columns sometimes grow to be huge structures.

Dissolve—To break down and mix into a liquid such as water.

Drapery—A calcite cave decoration formed when dripwater trickles along a sloping cave ceiling and builds downward into a delicate and colorful curtain of calcite.

Echolocation—A form of navigation that relies on sounds bouncing off obstructions back to the animal that made the sounds. It can be used in total darkness.

Flowstone—Limestone deposits formed when thin sheets of calcite build up on the floors and walls of a cave.

Guano—The excrement, or droppings, of bats in caves.

Gypsum—A mineral formed of calcium, sulfur, oxygen, and water.

Gypsum flowers—Cave decorations formed out of the mineral gypsum. They grow outward from their base, like toothpaste squeezed out of the tube, as delicate forms shaped like flower petals and curling stems.

Helictite—Curled, twisted, or spiraling and needle-shaped structures, usually made of calcite, in limestone caves. Usually, they are a few inches long.

Lava tube—A cave formed from a river of lava. The outside surface of the lava flow cools and hardens, forming a tube after the lava flow stops and the last molten lava in the interior flows out.

Magdalenians—The ancient people who created the paintings at Lascaux Cave.

Precipitate—When a mineral dissolved in water becomes solid and separates from the water; to come out of solution.

Rimstone dam—Calcite walls often formed in a steplike fashion along a sloping cave floor, each dam holding a pool of water. The water flows and tumbles from one pool into the next lower one.

Sandstone cave—A cave formed when water trickles down the face of a soft sandstone cliff and loosens and carries away part of the sandstone. Sandstone caves often served as dwellings for people living thousands of years ago.

Sea cave—A cave formed over centuries by the pounding action of ocean waves that loosen and break away rock particles.

Shaman—A tribal leader thought to have magical powers that enabled him to communicate with, or enter, the spirit world. A shaman looked after the social and physical well-being of his people.

Solution cave—A cave formed over thousands or millions of years as groundwater containing carbonic acid eats or dissolves its way through a massive block of stone and leaves many chambers with magnificent cave decorations.

Speleothem—Any limestone cave feature formed by mineral-rich dripwater, including stalactites, stalagmites, cave pearls, flowstone, and draperies.

Stalactite—An iciclelike formation on a cave ceiling; forms from calcite-rich dripwater falling from the ceiling.

Stalagmite—An upside-down iciclelike formation on a cave floor; forms from calcite-rich dripwater falling from the tip of a stalactite hanging above the stalagmite.

Water table—The top level of water stored in the ground.

For More Information

Books

Bendick, Jeanne. *Caves!: Underground Worlds*. New York: Henry Holt, 1995.

Heslewood, Juliet. *The History of Western Painting: A Young Person's Guide*. Austin, Tex.: Raintree Steck-Vaughn, 1996.

McFall, Christie. *America Underground*. New York: Cobblehill Books, 1992.

Silver, Donald M. *Cave*. New York: Scientific American Books for Young Readers, 1993.

Internet Resources

Answers to Frequently Asked Questions about Caving
http://www.cs.utk.edu/~doolin/cave/alt.caving.faq.html
http://www.mcs.net/~sford/web/caving_faq.html
These lists of answers to frequently asked questions about caving are excellent reading for anyone interested in exploring caves.

Commercial Caves of the United States
http://svis.org/comcaves/usacave.htm
A directory of show caves in the United States

National Caves Association
http://cavern.com/
This non-profit organization maintains a site listing of publicly and privately owned show caves and caverns in the United States.

National Speleological Society (NSS)
http://www.caves.org/
This is the Web site for the National Speleological Society (NSS), an organization serving cavers throughout the United States. At this site, you can locate local chapters (called grottos) of the NSS. The conservation policy is a code of conduct for cavers.

Speleo Link Page
http://hum.amu.edu.pl/~sgp/spec/links.html
This site lists lots and lots of links to cave-related Web sites around the world.

The United States Show Caves Directory
http://www.goodearth.com/showcave.html
This excellent site is a state-by-state directory of all the show caves in the United States. The site also features a "Virtual Cave" complete with photos and descriptions of many speleothems.

Index

About the Author

Roy A. Gallant has been called "one of the deans of American science writers for children" by *School Library Journal*. He has written more than eighty books for children on topics including astronomy, earth science, and evolution. He has written several books for Franklin Watts, most recently *Sand on the Move: The Story of Dunes* and *Geysers: When Earth Roars*. Mr. Gallant has worked at the American Museum of Natural History and been a member of the faculty of the Hayden Planetarium. He is currently the director of the Southworth Planetarium at the University of Southern Maine, where he also holds an adjunct full professorship. Mr. Gallant lives in Rangeley, Maine.